BULLETIN BOARD BONANZA

action bulletin boards to reinforce basic skills & concepts

DOROTHY MICHENER
and
BEVERLY MUSCHLITZ

illustrated by Beverly Muschlitz

ISBN 0-86530-028-3

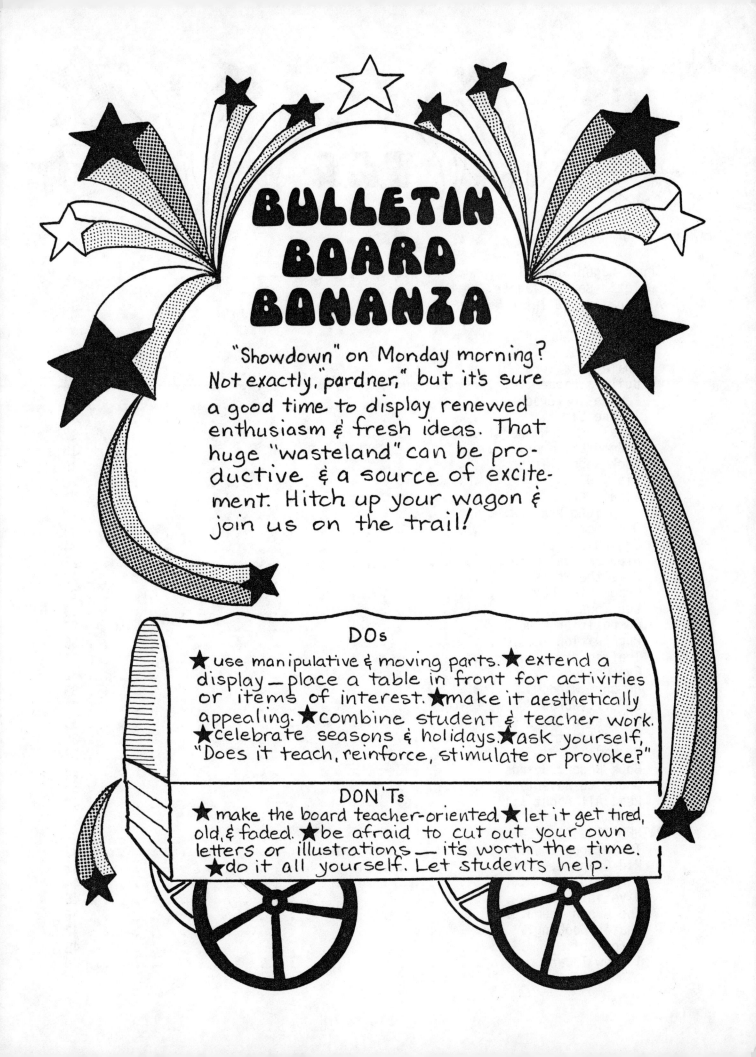

BULLETIN BOARD BONANZA

"Showdown" on Monday morning? Not exactly, "pardner," but it's sure a good time to display renewed enthusiasm & fresh ideas. That huge "wasteland" can be productive & a source of excitement. Hitch up your wagon & join us on the trail!

DOs

★ use manipulative & moving parts. ★ extend a display — place a table in front for activities or items of interest. ★ make it aesthetically appealing. ★ combine student & teacher work. ★ celebrate seasons & holidays. ★ ask yourself, "Does it teach, reinforce, stimulate or provoke?"

DON'Ts

★ make the board teacher-oriented ★ let it get tired, old, & faded. ★ be afraid to cut out your own letters or illustrations — it's worth the time. ★ do it all yourself. Let students help.

T.O.C.

CHUCK WAGON SPECIAL

BULLETIN BOARD NITTY-GRITTY

★★★ B.B. COVERINGS ★★★

A variety of materials may be used to cover your b.b. -- let your imagination go to work! You may want to try:
- ★ wallpaper ★ foil ★ burlap ★ maps
- ★ corrugated paper ★ newspaper
- ★ fabric ★ fishnets ★ tablecloths
- ★ kraft paper ★ individual construction paper sheets

★★★ B.B. BORDERS ★★★

Consider an attractive frame for your b.b.; it will provide an interesting focal point for student work or displays. Possibilities include: ★ paper chains ★ wallpaper borders ★ paper doilies ★ twisted crepe paper ★ paper plate flowers ★ adding machine tape with vegetable print stamp design ★ seasonal shapes ★ self-made folded cut-out patterns

★★★ EYE-APPEAL ★★★

Bulletin boards should be more than interesting display areas; bring them to life with brilliant colors, bold letters & an assortment of real objects & manipulative parts.

You may find it useful to enlarge drawings with an opaque projector. Tape paper on wall & draw lines with a pencil; then cut out & add color.

Achieve various dimensions by folding, rolling & pleating paper. Try to display all student work on contrasting paper.

★★ UNIQUE PAPER FRAME ★★

1. Fold 8½"×11" paper in half; cut diagonal slashes.
2. Open paper & fold each point back; staple or glue at the very end.
3. Be sure that the points do not lie flat -each should remain in a gentle curve to achieve a 3-D effect.

STEP 1

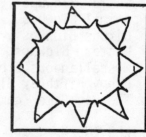

★★★ 3-D POCKETS ★★★

Provide manila folder pockets for materials to be attached to your b.b. These 6 easy steps will enable you to place a number of items in the pocket.

1. Open folder flat; fold along widest pre-scored lines.

2. Cut folded edge 1¼" from each side to create tabs.

3. Fold tabs in.

4. Crease & fold side edges on one side of folder (1¼").

5. Divide each fold in half with another <u>reverse</u> fold.

6. Staple folder together; tabs inside - outer fold flat on folder.

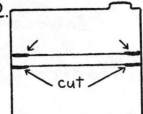
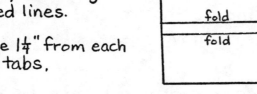
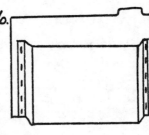
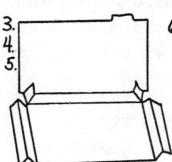
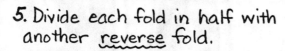

★★ STUDENT INVOLVEMENT ★★

Successful b.bs <u>must</u> have student input. Provide as many opportunities as possible for covering the board, making letters or helping with drawings or cutouts. Don't worry if it's not a perfect replica of what you had in mind-- the cooperative effort will draw enthusiastic use! Remember that some boards need to evolve slowly. Initial stimuli will often provide impetus needed for student work or activities.

★★★ ACTION BOARDS ★★★

Make your b.b. work for you! Hang up folders & bags with manipulative parts; add tables & floor displays. Provide an "annex"; gather materials, supplies, reference materials, special interest books & equipment. Students will stand in line to use an "action" b.b.! Carefully watch the use your boards get -- be sure to dismantle them one day before they "die"!

✸✸✸ LETTERING ✸✸✸

Interesting lettering announces that something important is happening at that spot! You need not be an artist -- just follow these simple suggestions.

1. Avoid precise, carefully drawn letters. Use a large felt marker to create a natural, irregular style. Outline with contrasting color for added interest.

2. Torn letters can provide an interesting look & can easily be constructed by students. Follow the folding technique described in #4 but do not cut. Remove "negative area" with little tears.

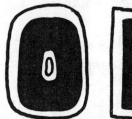

3. Try shadow lettering. Cut each letter needed from two contrasting colors of paper. Place one on top of the other with just a "shadow" of contrast shown in front of or behind the predominant color.

4. Bold letters cut from construction paper demand attention! You will find that most letters are symmetrical when divided in half. Folding precut rectangles or squares of paper makes cutting simple. Follow this format.

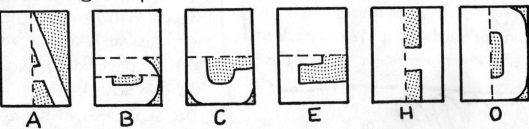

A   B   C   E   H   O

5. Standard materials for cut-out letters are fine, but why not try something different? ★foil ★fabric ★ yarn ★ wallpaper ★ newspaper ★ corrugated paper. Consider your theme -- use your imagination!

Bulletin Board Planner

I   Purpose

Teach - reinforce - illustrate - stimulate - enrich - apply - create

_____

_____

_____

II   Instruction

direct teaching - individualized - group process - research - discovery

_____

_____

_____

III   Process/Procedure

read & follow directions - respond to stimuli - manipulate parts - provide
student work/input - accompanying activity or ditto

_____

_____

_____

IV   Components

Title - instructions - learning activity - illustrations - parts

_____

_____

_____

V   Materials
Covering   _____
Title   _____
Cutouts   _____
Table   _____
Other   _____

VI   Sketch   (use other side)

9

ALTERNATIVE BULLETIN BOARDS

USE A REFRIGERATOR BOX FOR A 4-SIDED b.b. ___ or ⟶

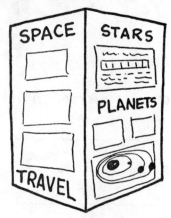

CUT APART AT ONE CORNER & STAND UP AS A ROOM DIVIDER — 8-SIDED B.B. !!

FILING CABINETS

TEACHER'S DESK

CLOSET DOORS

WINDOW SHADES

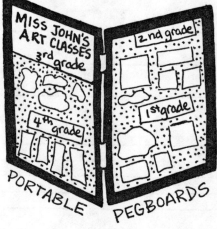

PORTABLE PEGBOARDS

BOOK SHELVES

ON THE LANGUAGE TRAIL

BULLETIN BOARDS HELP CREATE YOUR CLASSROOM'S ATMOSPHERE. MAKE IT ONE OF ENCOURAGEMENT, ENTHUSIASM AND CONFIDENCE!

Language arts skills permeate all that takes place in the early stages of a child's schooling. The following pages focus on these skills by providing boards that challenge students to read the headings; follow the directions; write specific assignments to be added to the board and shared with others; encourage reading and research; take part in group projects, and enjoy game-like tasks to reinforce learning.

"On the Language Trail" can help you to gather these skills together for effective learning. Let your bulletin boards assist in making YOUR classroom an inspiring place to learn.

SO, FOLLOW US DOWN THE LANGUAGE TRAIL!

OUR BOARD

SARAH'S SPACE · PAUL'S PLACE · JEAN'S JOTTINGS

SARAH · COLLECTION · BOB JANE · MY FRIENDS · SONG

PAUL · REPORT · AIRPLANES · AIRPLANE FACTS

MY FAMILY · MY HOBBY · MY PET · POEMS

PURPOSE

Provide each student with a b.b. section all his/her own--a great way to share personal interests & values!

 CONSTRUCTION

★ Section off the b.b.
★ Students select background, titles & items to be displayed.

USE

Rotate student b.b. sections on a weekly basis. Students will enjoy sharing momentos, photos, class work, hobbies, etc. Encourage all to look at the work & write a comment to the student.

WHALE of a WORD

1 syllable · cat · rose

2 syllables · apple · flower

3 syllables · patio · bicycle

4 syllables · television · geranium · FISH POCKET · FISH STORE (blank fish)

PURPOSE

Provide students practice in classifying words by syllables.

CONSTRUCTION

★ Make the whale from a large sheet of paper.
★ Cut out blue & green paper strips for waves.
★ Provide many paper fish; some with words of 1-4 syllables; some blank.

USE

Provide "starter" fish to be classified; then, let students use the dictionary to find additional words of 1,2,3 or 4 syllables. The words are written on the fish & tacked in the appropriate wave. Blank fish for student use may be placed in the "fish store" pocket.

★ Great for use with spelling or reading vocabulary words; a good source for creative writing stimuli!

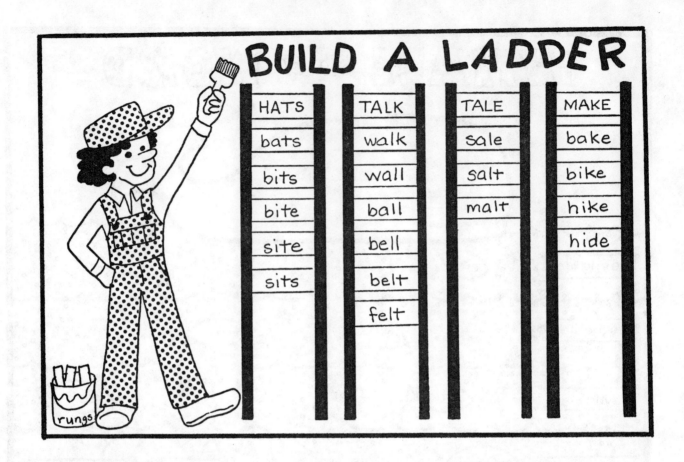

BUILD A LADDER

HATS	TALK	TALE	MAKE
bats	walk	sale	bake
bits	wall	salt	bike
bite	ball	malt	hike
site	bell		hide
sits	belt		
	felt		

rungs

PURPOSE

This individual or small group activity provides practice in word building.

CONSTRUCTION

★ Cut long paper strips for ladders & tack to b.b.
★ Cut strips of construction paper (a different color for each ladder) for "rungs" of the ladders.
★ Store "rungs" in paint bucket pocket.
★ Write one word at the top of each ladder.

USE

Have student change one letter in the last word on the ladder to make a new word. Student uses appropriate color "rung" to add to ladder. Work continues until ladder is full. Words may not be repeated. Be sure to change the top words regularly.

14

PERSON TO PERSON

WRITE YOUR NUMBER

CLASSROOM DIRECTORY

Andrews, John...764-7527
Baker, Susan..764-3619
Daniels, Tom....764-2001
Edmunds, Jean...764-3421

USING THE TELEPHONE

1. Listen for the dial tone.
2. Dial the number carefully.
3. Speak clearly.
4. Give your name.
5. Ask for the person you are calling.
6. Be courteous.

MAKE YOUR OWN DIRECTORY!

PURPOSE

Students use the telephone at an early age; provide practice in speaking & rules of courtesy.

CONSTRUCTION

★ Draw & cut out telephones; attach to b.b.
★ Attach real cord if available.
★ Write directions & directory on large sheets of paper.

USE

Have each student add name & telephone number to the b.b. directory. Provide speaking practice with toy telephones, or contact your local telephone business office for use of a classroom kit.

Small personal directories can be made — a good time to reinforce alphabetical order.

PURPOSE

Students "brown-bag-it" while learning the 5 "W's".

★ Attach 6 brown lunch bags labeled as shown to the b.b.

★ Place 5"x8" cards with sentences or paragraphs in "card" bag.

USE

Have students take cards from bag, read each & decide in which bag it belongs___ then "bag it." Have an answer card available for self-checking.

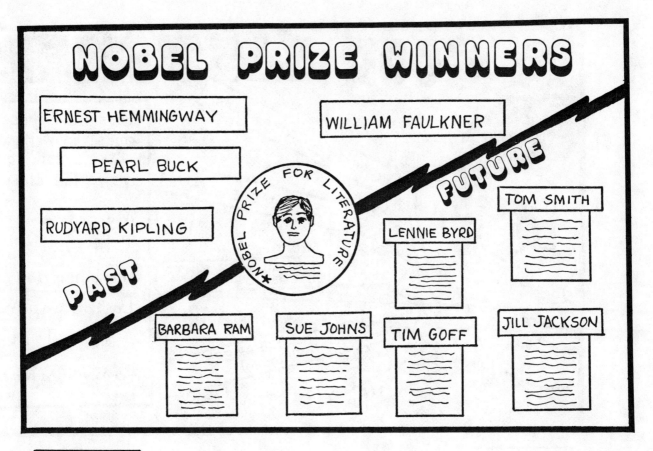

PURPOSE

Urge your students to perfect a composition so that it can be displayed on the "Nobel Prize" board.

CONSTRUCTION

★ Make construction paper rectangles for names of Nobel Prize winners.

★ Add student work.

USE

This b.b. can be kept up for an extended period of time if you change your classroom "Nobel Prize Winners" often. Encourage _every_ student to edit & rewrite work to be displayed. A good "cooperative corridor board."

PURPOSE

Remind your students of the rules for being a good listener — provide practice in use.

 CONSTRUCTION

★ Write classroom rules on the arrows.
★ Write directions on a poster board.

USE

After all students have written their 1-minute (or longer) talks, divide the class into small groups of 5. Have 1 student report while 2 listen, & 2 observe the listeners. How well did they follow the rules??

Change topics or activity several times during duration of b.b.

BOOK REPORT TREE

LEAVES

FLOWERS

PURPOSE

Stimulate the hesitant reader & writer.

CONSTRUCTION

★ Make a huge tree on your b.b.
★ Write each student's name on a branch.
★ Have students assist in making a large assortment of flowers & leaves.
★ Attach large pockets for leaves & flowers.

USE

Each time a book is read, have the student attach a mini-report "flower" to his/her branch. "Leaves" are added for each short story.

WATCH YOUR TREE BLOSSOM AND COME TO LIFE!!

Write a descriptive word in each petal. TITLE AUTHOR

TITLE AUTHOR Write a few descriptive sentences.

FISHY WORDS

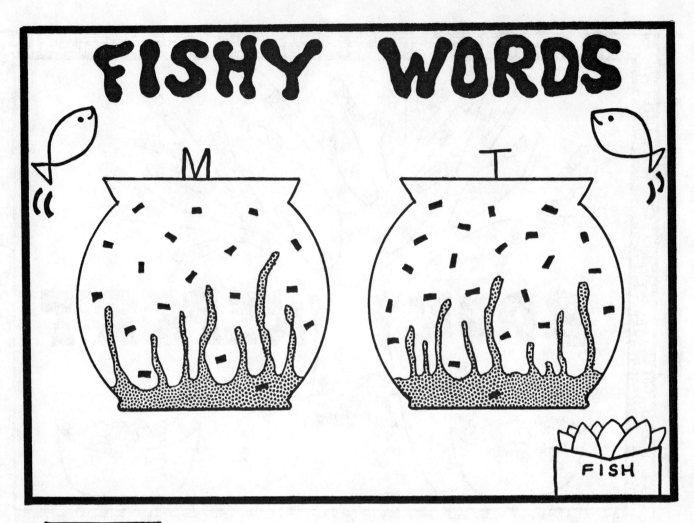

PURPOSE

Students reinforce recognition of beginning sounds by placing the "fish" on the proper bowl.

CONSTRUCTION

★ Make 2 large posterboard fishbowls.
★ Provide many posterboard fish, each with a picture.
★ Attach magnetic tape to fishbowls & back of fish.

USE

Student removes a fish from the pocket; looks at the picture on the fish & says the word for the picture. The fish is then placed on the fishbowl with the same beginning sound. ★Change letters on top of fishbowls weekly. You may want to use more than 1 sound. The fish may also be used for word endings.

noah's ark

The water is rising and you must get to the ark. Whom will you take with you; what 5 personal items will you bring? Write in the section of the ark assigned to you.

(STUDENT WORK AREA)

CONSTRUCTION

Enlarge ark using an opaque projector. Students color the animals. Divide boat into sections — one for each pupil.

USE

Students may illustrate as well as write in their individual areas. Use completed ark for discussion purposes.

Follow up: Have students write creative stories about the imaginary voyage.

JUMP into READING

PURPOSE A b.b. that provides book summaries & serves as a discussion starter.

CONSTRUCTION

★ Cut 2 life-sized poster board legs.
★ Put old socks & worn sneakers on legs.
★ Attach to b.b. with straight pins.
★ Provide footprint outlines for reports.

USE This creative visual stimuli will "move" students to write their book summaries. Encourage class to use the summaries for new book selections.

Also- may be used as a discussion starter:

• Where have these sneakers been?
• How did the socks get stained?
• How old was the person who wore these socks?

THE STORY OF WILLIE MAYS
This book tells about the life of Willie Mays; how he grew up and came to be a famous baseball player on a major league team.
Read to find out how his grandfather helped him and what Leo Durocher did for him.

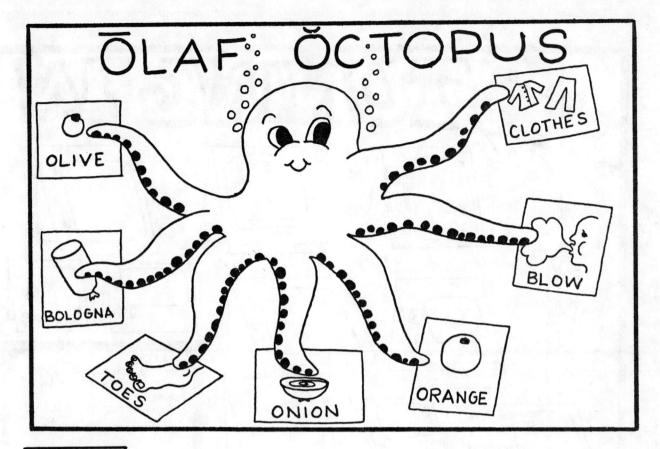

ŌLAF ŎCTOPUS

PURPOSE

This attractive display will entice youngsters & aid in the learning of long & short vowels.

CONSTRUCTION

★ Enlarge "Ōlaf" onto a large sheet of paper. Cut out & tack on b.b.
★ Make picture-word cards.

USE

Have students write the words for the pictures on a sheet of paper & mark the featured vowel (ŏ) long or short.

As the youngsters learn this vowel, change Olaf's name (April, Elmer, Ida, Ulysses) & the pictures.

Encourage students to add their own words to their lists of long & short vowels.

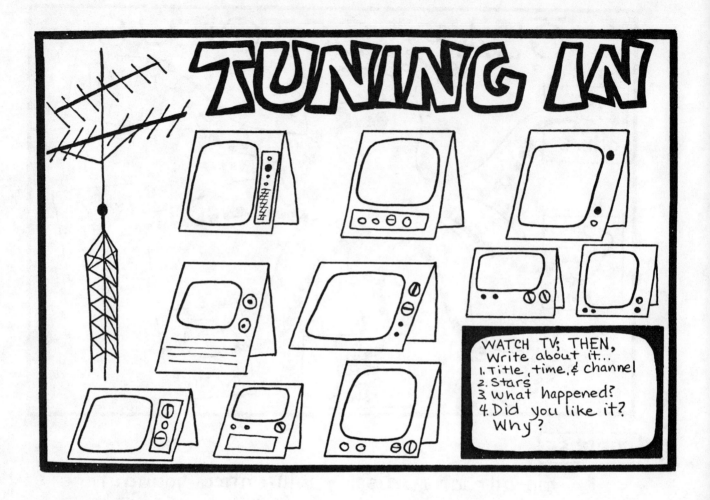

TUNING IN

WATCH TV; THEN,
Write about it...
1. Title, time, & channel
2. Stars
3. What happened?
4. Did you like it?
Why?

PURPOSE

Follow up at-home television viewing with a structured writing experience.

CONSTRUCTION

★ Make title & draw a simple TV tower..

★ Construct a large TV— write directions on screen.

★ Students use construction paper to make TV covers; then add lined paper & staple together to form booklets.

USE

Ask students to select a TV program carefully; encourage the use of a TV guide if possible. Have them take notes to refer to when writing. Students will be motivated to complete their work when they see the board begin to fill! Urge the class to read & react to each others work.

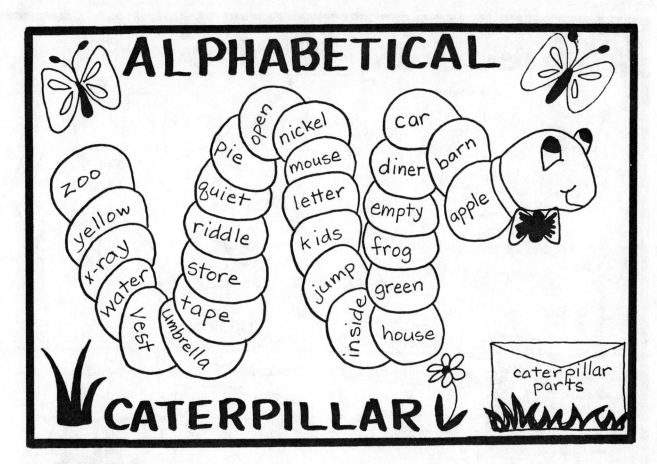

ALPHABETICAL CATERPILLAR

PURPOSE

Alphabetizing can be fun when students manipulate this cute, creepy, crawly caterpillar.

CONSTRUCTION

★ Cut out grass from green construction paper.
★ Make paper butterflies.
★ Cut a caterpillar head & segments from construction paper.
★ Add a pocket for caterpillar parts.

USE

Have student take caterpillar parts from pocket & tack them alphabetically to form a caterpillar. Student may arrange in any pattern desired.

A GOOD WAY TO REINFORCE WEEKLY SPELLING LISTS.

NAME THE NOUNS

PURPOSE

This easily changed, manipulative b.b. provides practice in identifying parts of speech.

CONSTRUCTION

★ Make a bold title. Write names of parts of speech on cards.
★ Draw the woman on a long sheet of paper.
★ Write vocabulary words on oaktag rectangles.
★ Make construction paper "X's" & place in pocket on b.b.

USE

Have student/s tack "X's" over the words that are nouns. Be sure to have an answer card available for self-checking.

This idea can be used for adjectives, verbs, etc. A good use for spelling or content area vocabulary words.

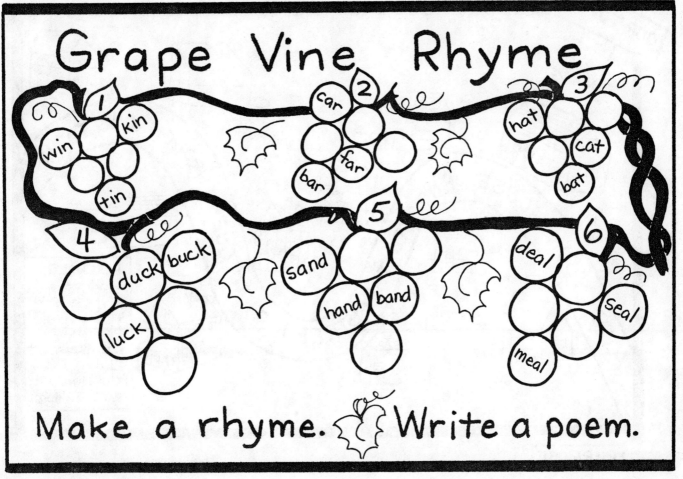

Grape Vine Rhyme

1. win, kin, tin
2. car, far, bar
3. hat, cat, bat
4. duck, buck, luck
5. sand, hand, band
6. deal, seal, meal

Make a rhyme. Write a poem.

PURPOSE

    Clusters of rhyming words provide the basis for a writing experience.

CONSTRUCTION

★ Make grapes from construction paper circles tacked together in a bunch. Write words on grapes.

★ Add leaves & vines.

USE

    Student directions: Number paper 1-6; then, write 3 additional rhyming words for each bunch of grapes. Select one bunch, & use all words in a poem.

WORDS SHOULD BE CHANGED OFTEN.

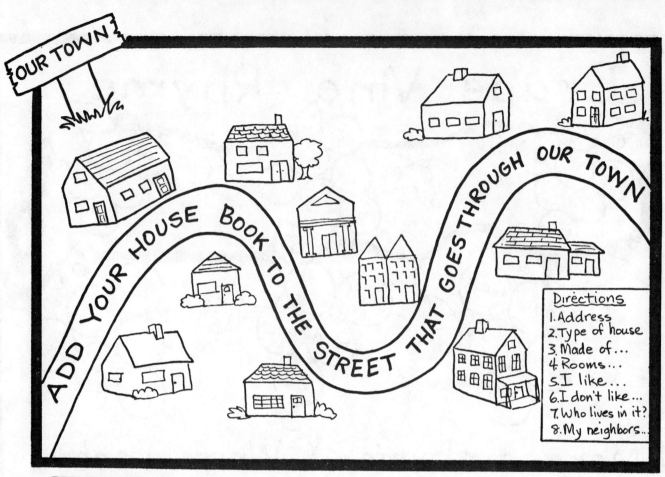

OUR TOWN

ADD YOUR HOUSE BOOK TO THE STREET THAT GOES THROUGH OUR TOWN

Directions
1. Address
2. Type of house
3. Made of...
4. Rooms...
5. I like...
6. I don't like...
7. Who lives in it?
8. My neighbors...

PURPOSE

Provide stimuli for students reporting on a familiar subject — their own homes.

CONSTRUCTION

★ Make poster board signpost.
★ Cover board with seasonal "ground" color.
★ Draw a road.
★ Add directions.
★ Provide construction paper & lined writing paper.

USE

Brainstorm a vocabulary list focusing on houses & neighborhoods.

Student directions: Make a house booklet telling about your house; write the address above the door. Be sure the cover illustration shows all features of the front view. Cut booklet shape accordingly.

PROVIDE OPPORTUNITIES TO SHARE!

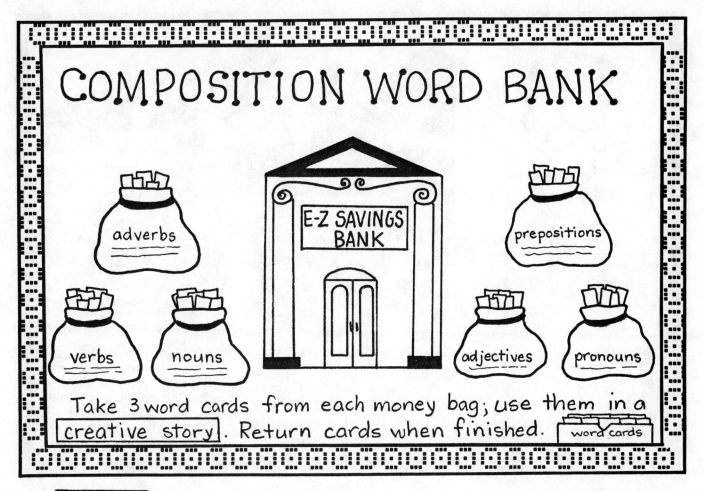

COMPOSITION WORD BANK

Take 3 word cards from each money bag; use them in a creative story. Return cards when finished.

PURPOSE

An attractive reminder & useful instructional tool for writing with specific kinds of words.

CONSTRUCTION

★ Make a large bank drawing.
★ Make poster board "money bags". Add parts of speech with brief definitions.
★ Provide vocabulary words written on 3"x5" cards to be classified into "bags" according to parts of speech.

USE

Have student directions on b.b.

Write the type of composition to be written on a separate card so it can be easily changed.

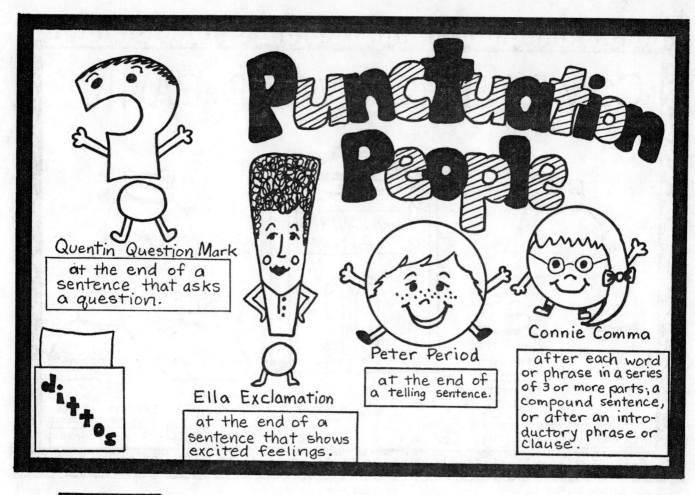

Quentin Question Mark
at the end of a sentence that asks a question.

dittos

Ella Exclamation
at the end of a sentence that shows excited feelings.

Peter Period
at the end of a telling sentence.

Connie Comma
after each word or phrase in a series of 3 or more parts; a compound sentence, or after an introductory phrase or clause.

PURPOSE

Students remember the rules of punctuation quickly with these whimsical characters.

CONSTRUCTION

★ Use posterboard for a bold title & "punctuation people."
★ Cut out large paper rectangles & write definitions on them.

USE

Have a ditto of unpunctuated sentences to be used in conjunction with this b.b.

LEAVE UP FOR ADDITIONAL REINFORCEMENT

PURPOSE

Provides practice in identifying blends; good use of visual memory.

CONSTRUCTION

★ Cut cars from white paper; add words.
★ Make a ditto sheet that corresponds to b.b. (Leave the cars on the ditto sheet blank.)

USE

Have students color all cars with the same blend one color. The cars on the b.b. must be in the same position as those on the ditto.
EASILY ADAPTS TO OTHER SKILLS!

PURPOSE

Introduce your class to the enticing descriptors used in advertisements.

CONSTRUCTION

★ Write brainstormed descriptors on b.b.
★ Cut out several good newspaper ads to use as examples; underline the "selling" words.
★ Rotate a display of student work.

USE

Brainstorm a class list of adjectives that may be used to sell a product; use these as a basis for the b.b. Have students choose 2 newspaper ads & underline the "selling" words. Assign a number of advertisements to be written by students, using b.b. superlatives as "starters."

HOMONYM WINDOWS

	1	2	3	4	5	6
1	see	real	beat	whole	ate	hare
2	red	won	feet	forth	eye	ant
3	blue	fair	lone	mail	gate	brake
4	maid	knot	dents	herd	kernel	night
5	hall	in	fare	altar	flee	hose
6	ail	ceiling	idol	heel	our	ade

across   down

PURPOSE

A multi-faceted language activity reinforcing sentence-writing & homonyms.

CONSTRUCTION

★ Divide a large sheet of kraft paper into 36 squares.
★ Number 2 sets of 2"x3" construction paper strips 1-6.
★ Add 2 pockets labeled "across" & "down" to hold number strips.

USE

Have students pick a number from either pocket. If number is chosen from the "across" pocket, student writes a sentence for each word in that row. If number is chosen from the "down" pocket, student writes a homonym & definition of each word. This grid can also be used diagonally from corner to corner. Have students use grid daily until several rows have been completed.

PURPOSE

To provide matching practice in various curriculum areas.

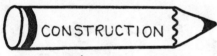 CONSTRUCTION

★ Use a colorful 14"x22" posterboard as a base for pockets.
★ Cut 12 library book pockets in half.
★ Attach photo corner to the lower corners of each pocket.
★ Provide strips of paper to slide into corners & 3½"x2½" cards to put into pockets for answers.

USE

Have students match answers to word pockets. This versatile b.b. can be changed many times using the basic board & photo corners — just change the title & add appropriate visuals.

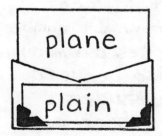  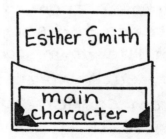 

WHAT'S IN THE SOUP?

ANSWER THESE QUESTIONS

1. What is the brand name and type of soup?
2. What company made the soup? What is its address?
3. How much did it cost?
4. List the ingredients in the soup.
5. Find 4 words on the label that you would like to learn. Write their definitions.

PURPOSE

To improve students' abilities to read for specific information, & to increase vocabulary skills.

CONSTRUCTION

★ Provide variety of soup labels.
★ Write questions on a large sheet of oaktag.
★ Add illustrations made from construction paper.

USE

Students select 4 different soup labels & answer the questions using the information on the chosen labels. To extend this activity, have students comparison shop in 3 different markets or compare the ingredients in the same kind of soup of different brands. Which is the better buy?

PURPOSE

Combine subject area vocabulary with classification skills.

CONSTRUCTION

★ Cut & paste construction paper together to make 6 cat faces.
★ Paste a library book pocket on each mouth.
★ Write words to be classified on 3"x5" cards
(ie. beet, dollar, lion, fear, carpenter, addition, pork, etc).
★ Add a large pocket for card storage.

USE

Students classify the word cards by putting them into the appropriate cat's mouth. Provide an answer card for self-checking.

Change the categories often — students may want to add to the pockets.

MY MAIL

PICK UP TIMES

paper

envelopes

People School
84 School Road
Grintown, Pa. 17602

Kelly Henry
1821 Hemlock Road
Happytown, Pa. 17603

PURPOSE

HELP YOUR YOUNG STUDENTS REMEMBER THEIR ADDRESSES BY "MAILING" THEMSELVES A LETTER.

 CONSTRUCTION

★ Make a mailbox from a large cardboard box. Decorate it & cut a slot.
★ Attach to b.b.
★ Tack up a large "envelope" showing the proper form for addressing.

USE

Ask each student to write a letter or draw a picture. Direct students to fold their finished work & place in business-size envelope. Have each child address the envelope to him/herself, and "mail" it in the "mail box."

☆ To heighten anticipation, deliver the mail about 1 week later. Listen to the giggles of delighted youngsters!

PURPOSE

To provide motivation for the reluctant reader.

CONSTRUCTION

★ Divide b.b. in half.
★ Let each student design a "promo" for his/her book report.
★ Provide table for student reports and/or displays.

USE

Tack up an intriguing notice prior to completion of board.

Do you know what Leslie's reading?

Student's board must display the Have you heard about Robbie's book? student's name & title of book along with any or all of the following:

★Illustration done by student ★Taped advertisement for the book ★Written book report ★Display of objects mentioned in the book (sneakers, basketball, trophy, etc) ★Art project related to book (diorama, puppet, book jacket).

WE GUARANTEE THAT AFTER THE FIRST STUDENTS ARE FEATURED, OTHERS WILL BE WAITING IN LINE WITH THEIR BOOKS!!!

DOORS TO ADVENTURE

PURPOSE

Young people love adventure! Encourage them to share their favorite stories with others.

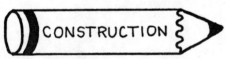 CONSTRUCTION

★ Make a large posterboard "door".
★ Staple it along one edge so that it can be opened.
★ Write student directions behind the door.
★ Attach 2 pockets to board. Put lined paper in one; in the other, put construction paper for students to use to make "door" covers for their booklets.

DIRECTIONS BEHIND DOOR

Read an adventure.
Write a report.
Follow these directions:
... Title
... Author
... Main characters
... Setting
... Plot
... High point of the adventure
... Was it exciting? Explain.

USE

Encourage each student to create a "door" that is compatible with the story read.

A good b.b. for corridor or cafeteria where students can read the reports.

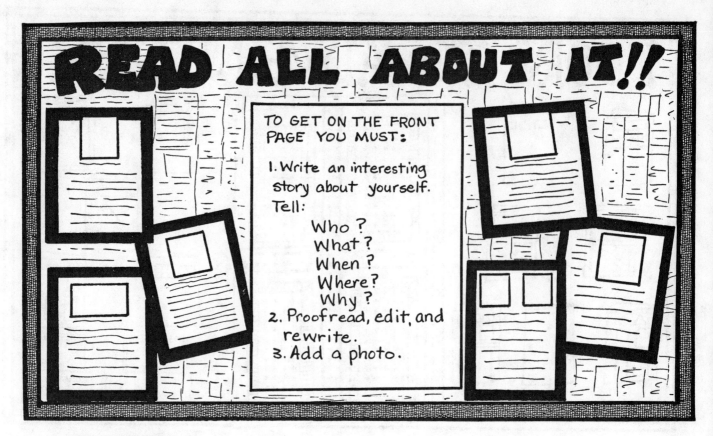

READ ALL ABOUT IT!!

TO GET ON THE FRONT PAGE YOU MUST:

1. Write an interesting story about yourself.
   Tell:
   - Who?
   - What?
   - When?
   - Where?
   - Why?
2. Proofread, edit, and rewrite.
3. Add a photo.

To provide students with an opportunity to write about themselves; to strengthen self-concepts & express feelings & values.

CONSTRUCTION

★ Completely cover b.b. with newspaper.
★ Make a bold title.
★ Add instructions.
★ Mount students' work on black paper & hang on b.b.

USE

Encourage students to read news stories, paying careful attention to the journalistic style used. Then, stress writing good leads, editing, proofreading & rewriting.

If a student doesn't have a photo of himself/herself, offer to take one, or suggest a self portrait.

Be sure to give your slower students extra support & guidance. The result will be a "front page story" for a proud youngster.

MATHEMATICS STAMPEDE

MANY PUPILS NEED MORE MATERIALS THAN CAN BE PROVIDED IN A TEXTBOOK. LET YOUR BULLETIN BOARDS FILL THAT GAP!

As you know, students require a variety of approaches to mathematics that appeal to different interests and abilities. The following pages are designed to provide that variety, along with a structure that will reinforce necessary concepts and skills.

When helping the slower learner achieve proficiency in computational skills, or providing average and better students additional opportunities, eye-catching bulletin boards can provide the additional resource needed. Even tedious drill can be exciting with an imaginative procedure!

WATCH OUT -- THE STAMPEDE
        IS ABOUT TO START!

TRASH GRAPH
CLEAN UP OUR WORLD

PURPOSE

To raise the consciousness level of your class with a "growing" reminder, and reinforce graphing.

CONSTRUCTION

★ Draw graph on a large sheet of paper.
★ Attach trash as shown with glue, tape or tacks.

USE

Take your students on a walk around your school yard or nearby community. Collect trash that is polluting their environment. Attach trash to graph for visual stimuli ie. soda cans & tabs, gum & candy wrappers, etc.

Repeat the trash walk weekly & continue to add to the graph.

Students' anti-pollution stories & observations could be added to board.

Kid graph

HOW MANY KIDS IN SCHOOL?

Kdg.	☺	☺	☺	☺	☺	☺	◖	
1st	☺	☺	☺	☺	☺	☺	☺	☺
2nd	☺	☺	☺	☺				
3rd	☺	☺	☺	☺	☺	☺	◖	
4th	☺	☺	☺	☺	☺	☺	☺	◖
5th	☺	☺	☺	☺	☺	☺	☺	
6th	☺	☺	☺	☺	◖			

PICTO-GRAPH KEY
☺ = 10 KIDS

PURPOSE

Pictorial representation is a good way to introduce graphing to your students. Simple mathematical relationships are easy to grasp when presented in this manner.

CONSTRUCTION

★ Draw a large grid.
★ Write the various notations on separate pieces of paper & tack on the board. The graph can then be used for other topics.

USE

Have students count the number of pupils in order to reinforce the concept of 1-10 ratio. Students can then make their own pictograph focusing on topics of personal interest.

OUR TRIP

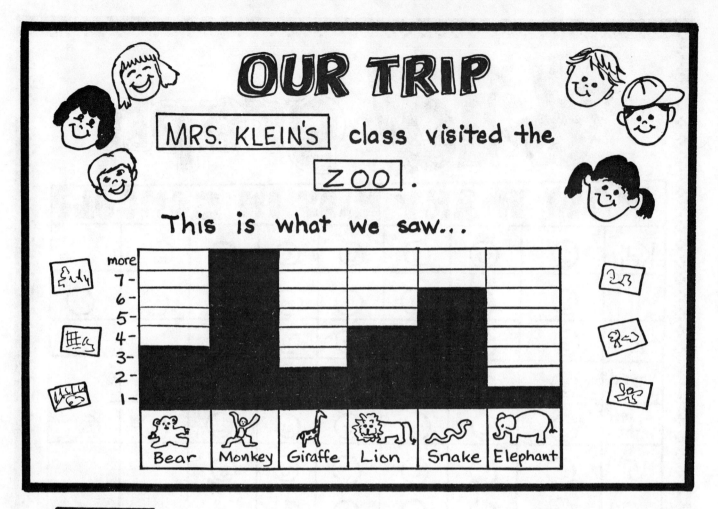

MRS. KLEIN'S class visited the ZOO.

This is what we saw...

(graph with animals: Bear, Monkey, Giraffe, Lion, Snake, Elephant — vertical scale 1 to more/7)

PURPOSE

To share a class trip through graphic representation.

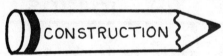 CONSTRUCTION

★ Construct a permanent b.b. background in a well-traveled corridor.

★ Add titles & basic written information. Leave blanks for teacher's name & type of trip.

★ Each group attaches a huge graph depicting an element of the trip.

★ Add photos.

USE

This versatile board can be used throughout the year by many classes. Students keep records on the trip, & then transfer this information to the b.b. Urge your colleagues to share this unique idea!

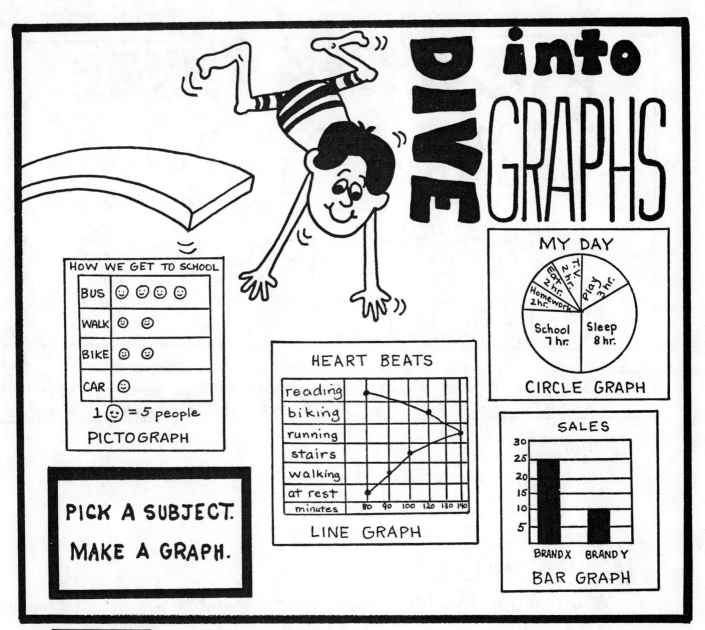

DIVE into GRAPHS

HOW WE GET TO SCHOOL

BUS	☺ ☺ ☺ ☺
WALK	☺ ☺
BIKE	☺ ☺
CAR	☺

1 ☺ = 5 people

PICTOGRAPH

PICK A SUBJECT.

MAKE A GRAPH.

HEART BEATS

reading
biking
running
stairs
walking
at rest
minutes   80 90 100 120 130 140

LINE GRAPH

MY DAY

T.V. 2 hr. / Eat 2 hr. / Homework 2 hr. / Play 3 hr. / School 7 hr. / Sleep 8 hr.

CIRCLE GRAPH

SALES

30
25
20
15
10
5

BRAND X   BRAND Y

BAR GRAPH

PURPOSE

To develop the concept of graphing as a picture of information that has been gathered.

CONSTRUCTION

★ Use commercial graphs or make your own.
★ Mount each graph on a different color of paper to avoid confusion.
★ Add the diver & title.

USE

Develop a simple graph with students; show how it summarizes information in a visual way.

THE GREEN THUMB
HOW DOES YOUR GARDEN GROW?

PURPOSE

A manipulative b.b. that can be used for many different matching skills.

CONSTRUCTION

★ Cut out a large hand with a green thumb as a visual stimulus.
★ Cut out flower stems (🌷). Add problems & attach to board.
★ Cut out a variety of flower shapes. Add answers & place in pocket on b.b.
★ Cut out vine shape with thick stems; write answers on it.
★ Cut out leaf shapes; write problems; place in pocket on b.b.

USE

Have students attach flower answers to stems & leaf facts to answer vine. Be sure students ask a friend to check answers.

What's Cooking?

ABBREVIATIONS IN THE KITCHEN

L. C. oz. lb.
kg. T. gal. g.
mL. tsp. qt. pt.

PURPOSE Reinforce student knowledge of measurements, abbreviations, & capacities through exploration.

CONSTRUCTION

★ Cut out construction paper rectangles. Write abbreviations on them.
★ Draw or cut out pictures of food.
★ Make the poster board "cook."
★ Provide a table with plastic cups, spoons, scale, rice or beans.

USE

Have students copy the abbreviations from the board, then write the words on a sheet of paper. Set up a table with the utensils (cup, tsp., qt., etc.). Students can compare sizes, or fill with rice or beans to compare capacities.

A GOOD INTRODUCTION TO A COOKING EXPERIENCE!

GERONIMO!

PURPOSE A progress b.b. to encourage memorization of math facts.

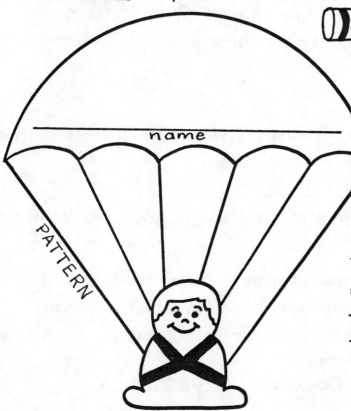

name

PATTERN

CONSTRUCTION

- Have students paint a b.b. sized mural as a background.
- Draw lines across to indicate levels.
- Students use pattern to make parachutes.

USE

Have each student tack a chute to 1ˢᵗ level of b.b. After each new set of math facts is learned & tested, students move chute to next level.

GERONIMO!

PURPOSE

Ordering numbers can be fun, especially when students manipulate the parts.

CONSTRUCTION

★ Cut railroad cars from bright construction paper.
★ Write numerals 1-10.
★ Attach engine (#1) permanently to the board.
★ Draw tracks to direct the line of cars.
★ If tacks are a problem at your grade level, attach strips of velcro to board & cars.

USE

Students can use the board individually or in small groups. Play simple games such as—"What comes next?" "What's missing?" "What is out of place?" etc.

49

STRETCH YOUR DOLLAR

COUPON BANK
PUT IN
ONE IN ～ ONE OUT
TAKE OUT

CHECK THESE MONEY SAVERS

SHOPPING LISTS

FOOD AD

PURPOSE

To help students understand economy while reinforcing basic math facts.

CONSTRUCTION

★ Collect food coupons for use with "shopping lists" & coupon "bank."
★ Write "shopping lists" (work cards) using weekly food ads & coupon discounts. Place in pocket on b.b.
★ Scatter coupons on board as visual stimuli.
★ Mount & attach a current food ad.

USE

Encourage students' families & others in school to take part in the coupon exchange. Unwanted coupons are placed in "bank"; needed ones drawn out, one for one.

Students use the food ads & coupons to solve the problems on the "shopping lists."

Change ad, lists & coupons weekly.

BATTER UP! HIT! YOU'RE OUT! PLAY BALL! HOME RUN! STRIKE!

TAKE ME OUT TO THE BALL GAME!

TODAY'S SPORTS PAGE

MATH CARDS

blank balls

PURPOSE

A multi-use b.b. to encourage reading the sports page & to apply computation & problem-solving skills.

CONSTRUCTION

★ Write title & baseball vocabulary. Add a player cut from construction paper.

★ Attach a sports page.

★ Write math problems related to the page & place in marked pocket.

★ Provide paper balls in a pocket for students to write baseball problems for classmates to solve.

USE

Prior to using the b.b., review a sports page together so that students can see the hidden math problems focusing on averages, runs, team placement, etc.

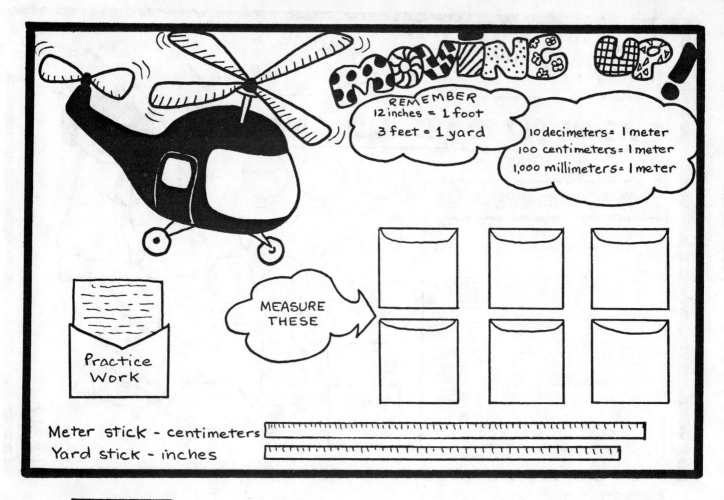

PURPOSE

To provide practice in measurement using inches & centimeters.

CONSTRUCTION

★ Attach a yardstick & meter stick to the b.b.
★ Write measurement equivalents.
★ Gather objects to be measured — i.e. Sheets of paper, mitten, scarf, etc. Place objects in manila envelopes & attach to b.b.
★ Make a pocket for worksheets or dittos.

USE

Use this b.b. as stimuli to introduce study of measurement. Place enrichment work in pocket for individual use.

PURPOSE

To help students achieve proficiency in computational skills & problem solving.

CONSTRUCTION

★ Cover b.b. with blue/green paper.
★ Drape a fishnet over b.b. in an attractive manner.
★ Have students draw, color & cut out various forms of sea life; attach under the net.
★ Cut out many fish shapes. Write math facts or problems on the fish. Hang on net with paper clips bent to resemble fish hooks.

USE

Color code the fish according to level of difficulty so that slower students will be successful, too. Have students copy work on paper. When problems are solved, students may want to exchange work for checking. Change fish regularly.

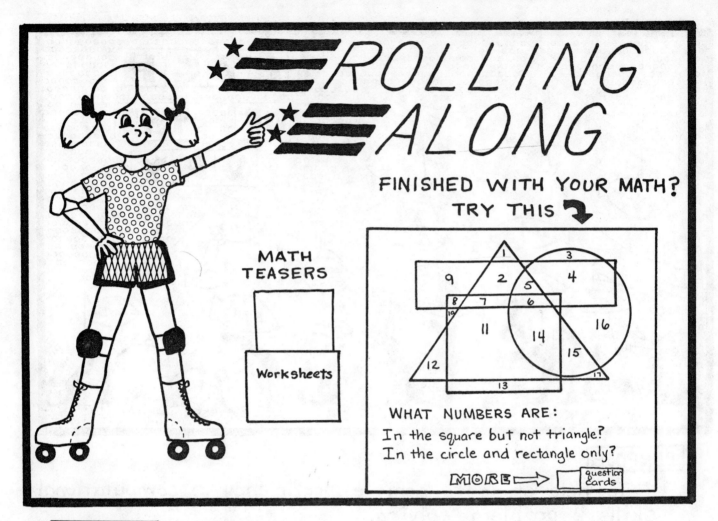

ROLLING ALONG

FINISHED WITH YOUR MATH?
TRY THIS ⟶

MATH TEASERS

Worksheets

WHAT NUMBERS ARE:
In the square but not triangle?
In the circle and rectangle only?

MORE ⟹ question cards

PURPOSE

To provide additional math suggestions for students that have finished assigned work.

CONSTRUCTION

★ Cover b.b. with paper. Add title & skater.
★ Make pocket for dittos or worksheets.
★ Make a large visual problem on posterboard.
★ Paste a small pocket for questions & answer card onto poster board.

USE

Students will use this board if you include work that is fun, yet purposeful. A good way to challenge the gifted! Be sure to change the problem frequently.

HOP-SKIP-JUMP

Rodney Rabbits starts at 0 and jumps three spaces at a time. Where will he be after 3 jumps?

hard cards

medium cards

easy cards

PURPOSE

To study the commutative property of multiplication through the use of the number line.

CONSTRUCTION

★ Draw title & number line.
★ Construct Rodney from posterboard.
★ Make 3 pockets for number line problems. Label & attach to board as shown.
★ Write easy, medium & hard problems on 3"x5" cards. Place them in the appropriate pockets.
★ Enlarge one problem on a posterboard to stimulate interest; change card often.

USE

Use b.b. to reinforce classwork. Encourage students to start with easy cards & work up to the harder ones. Provide an answer sheet for self-checking.

MRS. MULLIGAN'S MAGNIFICENT MATHEMATICIANS AT WORK

STOP

ONE WAY

1 → 2

3 → 4

CAUTION
work area ahead

SELF CHECK-UP
1 2 3 4

DIRECTIONS

BONUS 3 ← BONUS 2 ← BONUS 1

DETOUR

EXIT

PURPOSE

To structure use of predetermined work pages by means of an open-ended math b.b.

CONSTRUCTION

★ Make 6 3-D pockets (see instructions p. 10).
★ Make simple road signs.
★ Provide book pockets for self check-up.
★ Add directions.

USE

Pockets may contain daily worksheets or ditto pages in varying degrees of difficulty.

Time, elements, number of pockets & skills may be changed as needed. Self check-up should take place prior to the student's moving ahead to bonus pockets. Some students may not get to bonuses — that's OK!

LASSOING HEALTH, SCIENCE & SOCIAL STUDIES

Looking for something special to "rope" your students' interest in these areas? This section will help you develop pertinent, thought-provoking room displays that not only please the eye, but also provide for active learning.

The care, development & use of the total resources of our nation -- & of the world -- will soon be entrusted to today's students. As a teacher, you can help them develop a sense of responsibility to & understanding of self & society, of their environment & of their world. The ideas we've suggested here, combined with your special interests & teaching style, will give students an eager interest in & concern for present & future life on earth.

Now, sit straight in your saddle & dig in your spurs! Let these "ranch hands" help you lasso health, science & social studies.

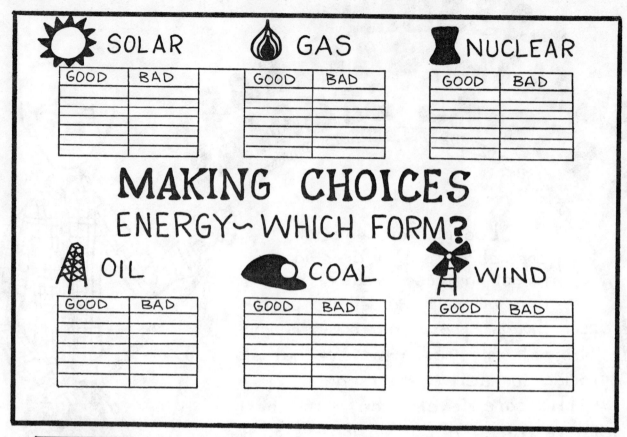

MAKING CHOICES
ENERGY~WHICH FORM?

SOLAR | GAS | NUCLEAR | OIL | COAL | WIND

Each with GOOD / BAD chart columns.

PURPOSE

Focus on a critical issue, & provide bulletin board stimuli for research & thinking out specific alternatives.

CONSTRUCTION

★ Create construction paper symbols.
★ Make oaktag charts for reporting.

USE

After each group has reported to the class, the pros & cons of each choice may be listed on the board. The completed b.b. provides a wealth of information for writing, discussion & decision-making projects.

This simple format can provide a vehicle for exploration of various current issues.

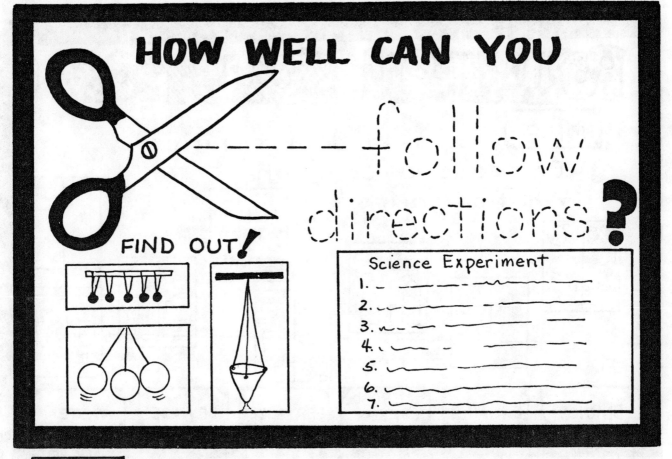

HOW WELL CAN YOU follow directions?

FIND OUT!

Science Experiment
1.
2.
3.
4.
5.
6.
7.

PURPOSE

Following written directions, step-by-step, is an important life skill to be developed & nurtured. Integrate this activity into your science curriculum.

CONSTRUCTION

★ Attach a question to be solved or an illustration.
★ Write directions in simple language.
★ Place a small table or desk adjacent to the board.
★ Provide all equipment necessary for the experiment.

USE

Permit students to conduct the experiment during free time. Control the number working at the table by limiting the chairs. Leave the basic board up for a few weeks, but change directions & experiments often.

POLLUTION SOLUTION!

NOISE is a kind of pollution.
It needs a solution!
What's yours?

SMOKE   EXHAUST   AEROSOL SPRAY   FERTILIZER   SEWAGE   WASTE

PURPOSE

To provide opportunities for students to explore various solutions for major environmental problems during a seven-week period.

CONSTRUCTION

★ Make a bold title & write a statement.
★ Write pollution words on separate cards. Attach to b.b. with photo corners or place in pockets.
★ Student pages are made by folding 9"x 12" paper in half. Label sides "pollution" & "solution." After student completes picture and/or statement, attach to b.b.

USE

Focus on one form of pollution per week; move that card to top of board. Provide time for group discussion & research prior to "solution" work. At the conclusion of the project, vote on best solutions. Write about them in school or community newspaper.

★ example

DAILY WEATHER LOG

(month) _____

	SUNDAY	MONDAY	TUESDAY	WEDNESDAY	THURSDAY	FRIDAY	SATURDAY

Partly sunny

snowy

hot

cold

sunny

cloudy

rainy

sleet

PURPOSE To learn to keep a log by observing & recording weather daily.

Use opaque projector to enlarge & copy.

CONSTRUCTION

USE Students take turns writing in dates & drawing the correct symbols. A good device to discuss concepts such as "yesterday", "tomorrow", & days of the week.

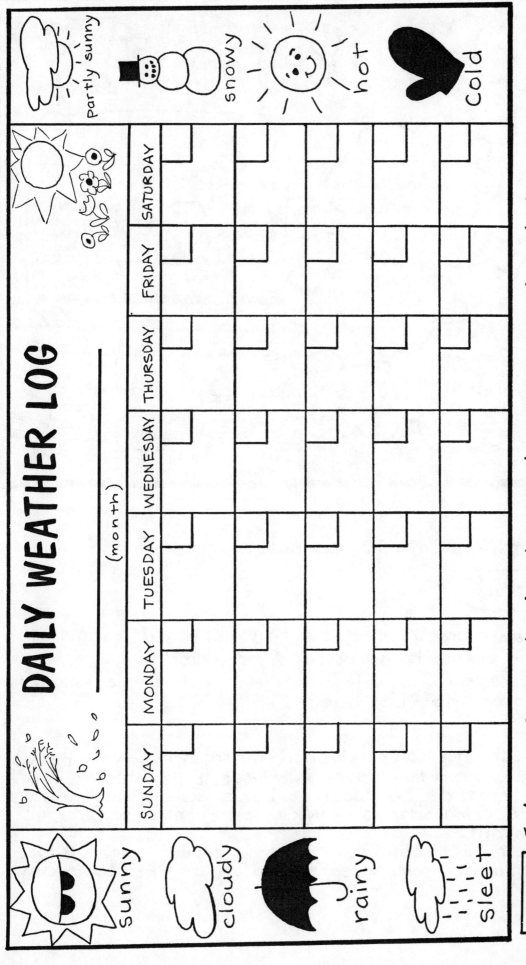

61

SCHOOL BUS SAFETY

We always remain seated while the bus is moving.

We keep our hands and heads inside the bus.

We do not bother the bus driver.

We do not yell or make a lot of noise on the bus.

We do not bother other people on the bus.

We do not eat on the bus.

PURPOSE

To remind students of bus safety rules.

CONSTRUCTION

★ Draw a large, colorful bus on posterboard or enlarge this one with an opaque projector.
★ Make smoke puffs for rules, putting the smallest closest to the bus.

USE

Several activities can be planned in conjunction with this b.b.
1. Invite a school bus driver into class to be interviewed.
2. Create student-made school bus safety mobiles.
3. Write compositions — "Why school bus safety is important."
4. Class project — construct a large papier mâche school bus; paint & write safety rules on the outside.

BICYCLE SAFETY

USE REFLECTORS AND LIGHTS.

USE HAND SIGNALS.

DON'T CARRY RIDERS.

OBEY TRAFFIC SIGNS.

RIDE ON THE RIGHT.

PURPOSE

To teach & reinforce bicycle safety.

CONSTRUCTION

★ Using an opaque projector, enlarge bicycle. Trace it onto b.b. paper.
★ Write safety rules on construction paper.
★ Add "grass" trim.

USE

Have youngsters create a collage incorporating pictures & drawings of bicycles & the rules of safety. Students can provide additional rules learned as a result of research.

PURPOSE

To have a lasting positive influence on eating behavior.

CONSTRUCTION

★ Make a "wanted" poster.
★ Make a food group chart or use a commercial one. Attach as shown.
★ Construct a pocket to hold paper plates.

USE

Introduce nutrition information & discuss food groups. Focus at least one lesson on each meal: breakfast, lunch, dinner & snack. Have students draw or paste food pictures on plates & tack onto b.b.

OUR REFRIGERATOR

I. Top Shelf
   A. Milk
   B. Soda
   C. Juice
   D. Ketchup
II. Second Shelf
   A. Cake
   B. Cheese
   C. Jelly
   D. Noodles
   E. Meat Drawer
      1. hamburger
      2. chicken
      3. hot dogs
III. Third Shelf
   A. Eggs
   B. Mustard
   C. Relish
   D. Pineapple
IV. Bottom Shelf
   A. Fruit
      1. apples
      2. oranges
      3. lemon
   B. Vegetables
      1. lettuce
      2. celery
      3. carrots
      4. cucumbers

PURPOSE

To teach outlining skills using simple, everyday subject matter.

CONSTRUCTION

★ Draw a huge refrigerator on b.b. paper.

★ Staple a door to the refrigerator so that it can be opened.

★ Have students make food items from construction paper & glue them in the refrigerator.

USE

After refrigerator has been "stocked," list items on each shelf using an outline format. Have each student make an outline of the contents of his/her home refrigerator; then, apply the outlining skill to another familiar item. Research or write a news article about it.

This b.b. is ideally suited for a closet door & can be done on a long strip of kraft paper.

STEPS TO A HEALTHY YOU

1. EAT THE RIGHT FOODS

2. EXERCISE

3. GET PLENTY OF SLEEP

SAMPLE LOG

	foods I ate today	exercise	# of hrs. slept
MON.			
TUES.			
WED.			
THURS.			
FRI.			
SAT.			
SUN.			

LET'S "KEEP IN STEP" TO STAY HEALTHY! Keep a log of your food, exercise and sleep for 1 week.

PURPOSE

To help youngsters evaluate their lifestyles through the use of a log.

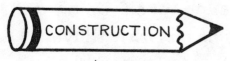 CONSTRUCTION

★ Use an opaque projector to aid in drawing the three figures.
★ Add title, numbers & sub-titles.
★ Make sample log on a large sheet of oaktag.

USE

Have students make logs on 12"×18" sheets of oaktag. Each day, the foods eaten, types of exercise & number of hours slept should be recorded. Provide time to analyze & share information. After learning more about good health, students may repeat the activity to compare changes & growth.

OUR PICNIC
WHAT ARE YOUR FAVORITES?

FOOD GROUPS CHART   **CALORIE COUNTER**   **MAKE A MENU**

PURPOSE

To plan a school picnic that provides a balanced meal based upon growth, health & energy needs.

 **CONSTRUCTION**

★ Cover b.b. with an old tablecloth.
★ Make & attach titles & pockets.
★ Have students add paper plates on which they have drawn pictures of their favorite foods.

USE

A spring picnic can be the stimulus needed to consider planning for good nutrition. Provide time for group work using calorie counters & food groups chart. An "off season" picnic can be fun — spread out the blankets, bring out the food & enjoy.

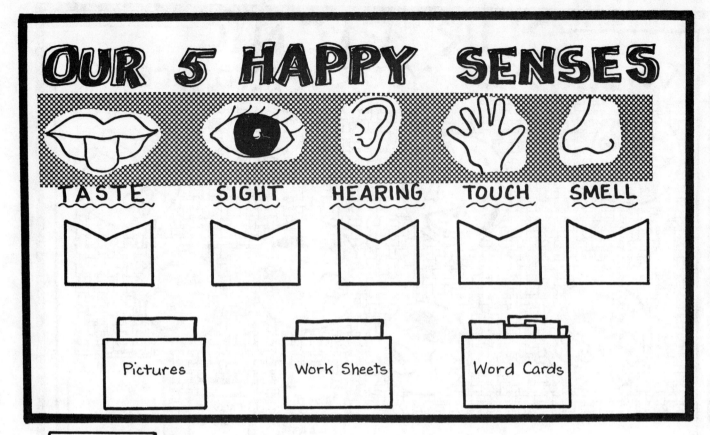

OUR 5 HAPPY SENSES

TASTE   SIGHT   HEARING   TOUCH   SMELL

Pictures   Work Sheets   Word Cards

PURPOSE

To help students become more aware of the pleasure they receive through their senses.

CONSTRUCTION

★ Draw symbols & label each of the senses.
★ Attach a pocket under each illustration.
★ Add 3 more pockets. Label one each for pictures, worksheets & word cards.
★ Cut photographs from magazines. Place in pocket.
★ Make a simple worksheet with sentence starters: "I am happy when I hear..." etc. Place copies in pocket.
★ On 3"x5" cards, write various descriptive words, ie. "sweet," "sour," "loud," etc. Place in pocket.

USE

Have students:
1. Classify pictures into appropriate pockets (ie. lady eating cake – taste).
2. Complete worksheets.
3. Classify descriptors on word cards into 5 categories & make a list of their classification.
4. Use b.b. & vocabulary for discussion.

68   Construction

The STUDENT DISPLAY

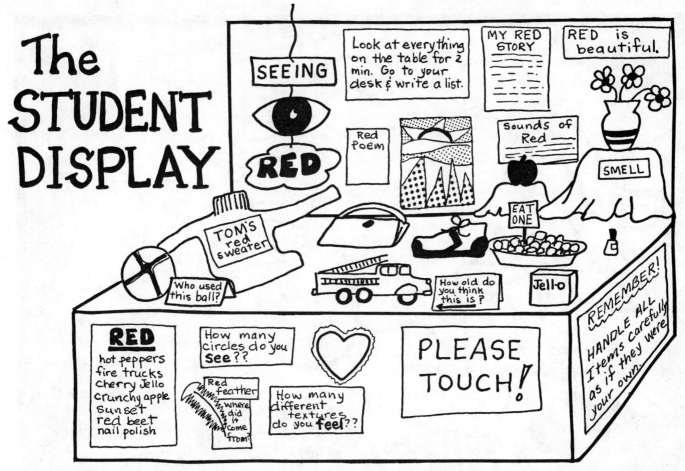

Combine a bulletin board, display table & collection of related objects into a bombardment of the 5 senses. Use of the Student Display provides opportunities for discussions, writing, art, math, reading, & aesthetic appreciation.

TO SET UP A DISPLAY

Decide on a central theme, ie. color, season, period of history, toys, environment, etc. Bring in a few items to stimulate interest; ask students to contribute. Arrange an attractive background & display table. Use burlap or old table cloths to drape over boxes on various levels to provide varied heights— all child level. Make a sign or mobile. Arrange items carefully. Attach word cards & attention getters.

TO USE A DISPLAY

Develop activity cards directing students to explore using their 5 senses. Write stories, poems— do math or research. Students will get involved, & add their own work —all focusing on the topic. Be sure to allow for freedom of choice & interest.

YOU MAY WANT TO LABEL ITEMS FOR PRIMARY STUDENTS

Write about jobs you do to help at home.

PURPOSE

To instill a sense of responsibility & cooperative effort.

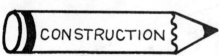 CONSTRUCTION

★ Draw a large web on the board.
★ Cut out a large, colorful spider.
★ Write a job on each leg.
★ Add student name, written on a card, to each leg.

USE

Discuss job responsibilities for home & school. Change helpers & writing assignment weekly to provide an opportunity for all to participate. Hang finished assignments around frame of b.b.

DEGREES OF IMPORTANCE

100° most important

75° very important

50° average importance

25° not very important

0° unimportant

WHAT ARE YOUR FEELINGS?

★ Draw a thermometer.

★ Select 10 cards.

★ Mark a temperature reading for each.

PURPOSE

To encourage students to consider the importance of various aspects of their lives.

CONSTRUCTION

★ Draw a large thermometer on the b.b.
★ Add instructions & a title.
★ Write many items on 3"x5" cards, ie. friendship, report card, religion, family, clothes, health, TV, money, sports, college, music, home, reading, etc.
★ Attach a pocket for cards.

USE

Provide time for each student to complete the activity (see directions on b.b.). Use personal thermometers as basis for group discussions. Be sure to compare likes & differences. Word cards may also be used as story starters.

VIP

PURPOSE

Every one of your students is a V.I.P. Take time to honor them all.

★ DAILY GAZETTE ★

HILLTOWN, U.S.A.

V.I.P. of week

★ SPOTLIGHT ★
on John Smith

Sports Highlights

Human Interest

Hobbies

Awards

Jobs

Friends

Movie Favorites

Likes

Dislikes

John's drawing.

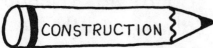 CONSTRUCTION

★ Cover board with pages from a newspaper.
★ Add a bold title.
★ Attach the V.I.P. picture.

USE

Have your students interview & write articles about the V.I.P. You might even add some of his/her work, a message from Mom, piece of artwork, etc. Focus on a different student every week or two. Kids will be proud to take this home as a memento!

WISE BIRDS give a hoot!!

★ OUR RULES ★

1. We follow directions.
2. We stay in our seats.
3. We raise our hands.
4. We put things away.
5. We take care of books and other things.
6. We respect the property of others.
7. We get to class on time.
8. We are polite to people.
9. We bring to class the things we need.

PURPOSE

To involve students in developing a list of expected school behavior.

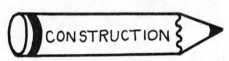

CONSTRUCTION

★ Draw & cut out owl.
★ Add title.
★ Develop rules. Write them on a piece of large posterboard that can be easily removed.

USE

Brainstorm a list of classroom rules with your students. Be sure to eliminate the unnecessary & unenforceable! Refine & rewrite in <u>positive</u> language. Post the rules on your b.b.; use for discussion purposes.

Move rules chart elsewhere to provide space for student-written work dealing with behavior & responsibility.

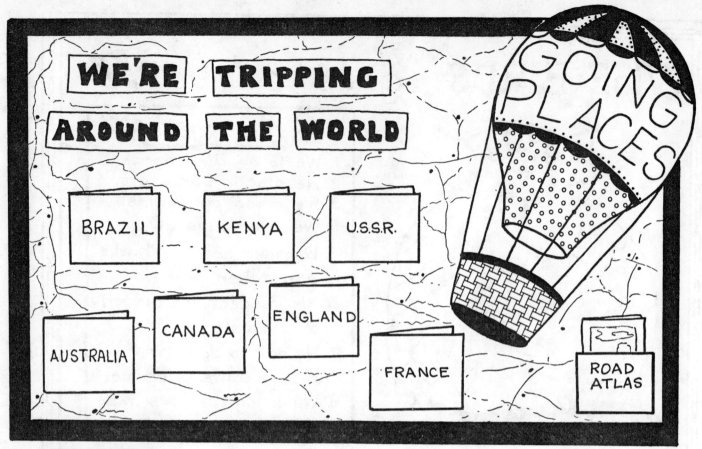

PURPOSE

To learn about the world through imaginary travel; integrate research, letter writing, math & composition skills.

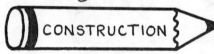

CONSTRUCTION

★ Cover b.b. with old road maps.
★ Attach a pocket for an atlas.
★ Add a large hot air balloon as visual stimulus.

USE

Have your class use the road atlas to plan an imaginary trip. Encourage them to estimate mileage, plot overnight lodging & sites to visit along the way. Incorporate all work, letters, diaries, etc. into a student-made folder. Attach folders to b.b. as completed.

THE ROUNDUP

Add a mixture of sagebrush & tumbleweed to your bulletin boards, & they will no longer be the bane of your existence!

This chapter is a collection of assorted ideas to reinforce skill development & encourage self-expression. The "Blowups" are single-page thematic illustrations that will add punch to your ideas. Simply enlarge the drawings using an opaque projector. Our bulletin board "Visuals" are self-explanatory pages, two to a theme. Check 'em out -- you'll find them useful on your trail!

In view of escalating costs, tightening budgets & emphasis on skills, practical approaches to learning are essential. That's just what you'll find in this section. You'll be proud to put your "brand" on these teacher-tested action boards. So saddle up & join us for the round up!

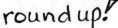

MAIL CALL

greeting

heading → 415 North St.
Bellmore, Kansas 62489
August 10, 1981

Dear Jack,

message → I will be visiting my aunt next week and I would like to see you then. We always have fun together.

Will you please write and let me know.

closing → Your friend,
Stuart

signature

LETTERS TO READ

PRACTICE PAPER

GOOD PAPER

word cinquain
a poem with 5 lines

Line 1 – one word; a person, place or thing
Line 2 – two words that tell about the first
Line 3 – three words that tell how the first word moves or acts
Line 4 – four words that tell something special about the first word
Line 5 – one word – another word to describe line one.

Butterfly
Winged rainbow
Fluttering through flowers
Gently through the meadow
Beauty

 write yours

MONKEY AROUND WITH SPELLING

DON'T FORGET
1. Read the words.
2. Look them up.
3. Use each word in a sentence.
4. Write the spelling words in alphabetical order.

WEEKLY LIST

turtle	please
brown	mouth
uncle	brother
yellow	should
slide	friend

CHOOSE ONE

Use all words in a story. OR Write a letter using all words OR Make a spelling game OR Your idea! check first.

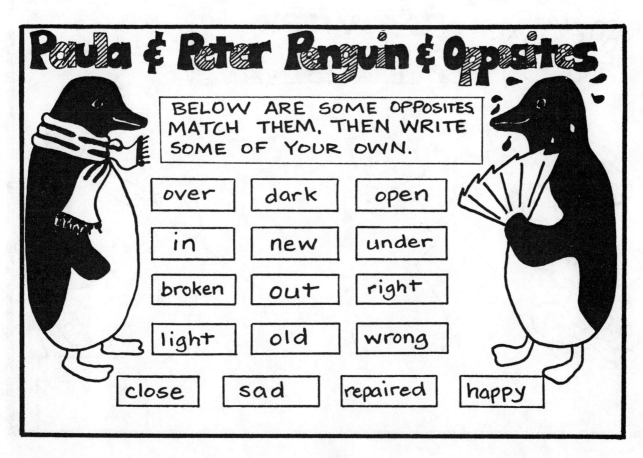

Paula & Peter Penguin & Opposites

BELOW ARE SOME OPPOSITES MATCH THEM, THEN WRITE SOME OF YOUR OWN.

over	dark	open
in	new	under
broken	out	right
light	old	wrong

| close | sad | repaired | happy |

77

"LOVE TO READ" POCKETS

mystery

nonfiction

plays

biography

poetry

fiction

science fiction

history

short stories

ADD YOUR REPORT ★ READ OTHERS

FLY WITH READING

PICK A PATTERN

MAKE A BOOKLET

WRITE YOUR REPORT

PATTERNS

WE READ THE NEWSPAPER

SHARE YOUR STORY

PASTE IT ON THE NEWSPAPER

1. Remove all real estate ads from pocket. Rank them in order from most expensive to least.

2. How much difference is there between the most expensive house and the least expensive?

3. Mr. and Mrs. Jones want a house for $55,000 - $65,000. How many can you find?

4. Pick a house ad and write a paragraph telling why you would like to own it.

5. Write a newspaper ad for your house and a neighbor's house.

'HOUSE FOR SALE' ADS

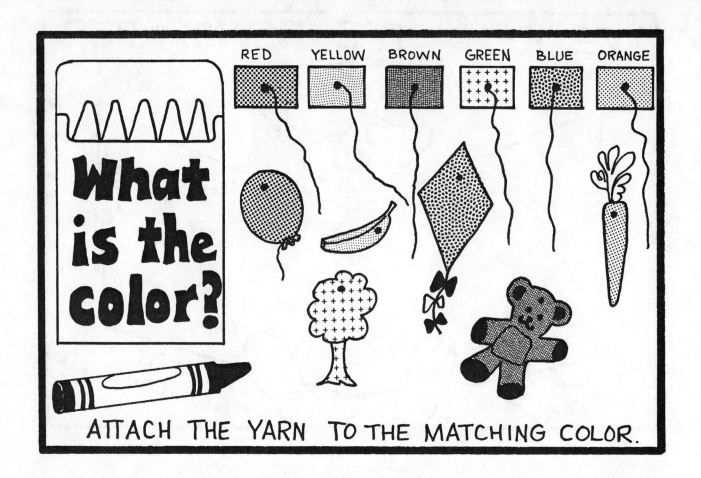

RED YELLOW BROWN GREEN BLUE ORANGE

What is the color?

ATTACH THE YARN TO THE MATCHING COLOR.

PLAYGROUND KNOW-HOW

PLACE THE:

1. red child on the <u>top</u> step.
2. blue child <u>under</u> the slide
3. green child on the <u>bottom</u> step.
4. yellow child at the <u>end</u> of the slide.
5. orange child on the <u>middle</u> step.

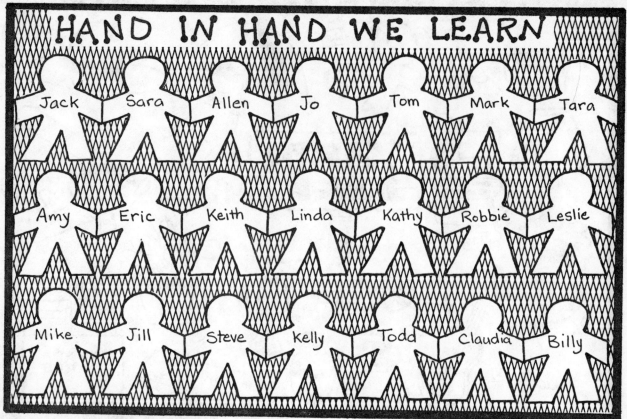

BACK TO SCHOOL

Take a shirt or pair of jeans. Write your name on it, color it and hang it on the line.

winter

spring

Summertime

CIRCUS

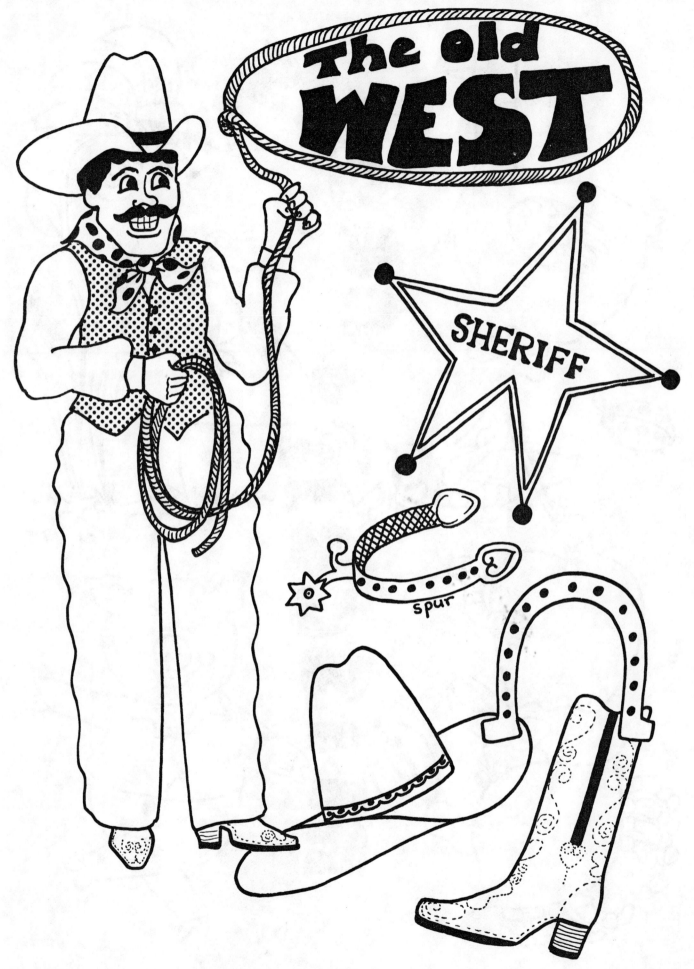

The Old WEST

SHERIFF

spur

miscellaneous

HAPPY BIRTHDAY TO YOU

THIS BULLETIN BOARD IS A GREAT INTRODUCTION FOR THE NEW STUDENT OR TO A NEW SCHOOL YEAR. EVERYONE IS SPECIAL, AND EVERYONE BELONGS ON THIS CAKE. (DON'T FORGET ANY MAINSTREAMED STUDENTS YOU MAY HAVE.) THIS IS ALSO A GOOD WRITING OR DISCUSSION STARTER.

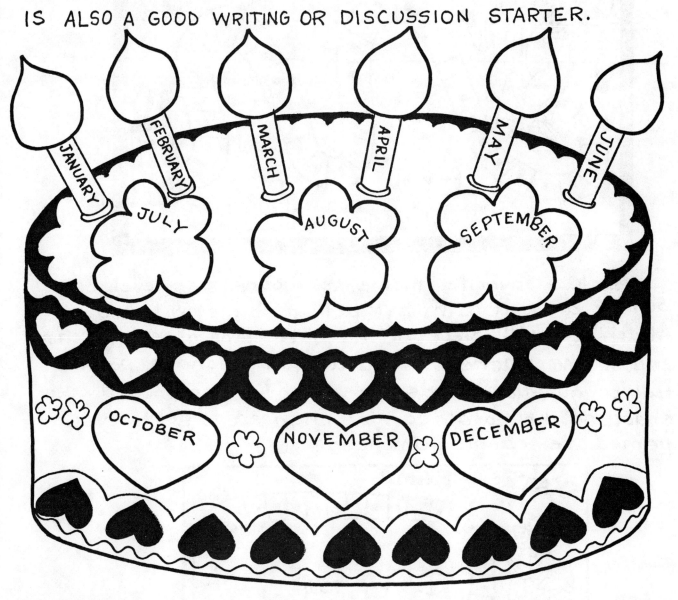

★ To enlarge for your bulletin board, use an opaque projector and add brilliant color.

the BIG game

CREATE A SUPER GAMEBOARD/LEARNING EXPERIENCE ON YOUR BULLETIN BOARD. YOUR STUDENTS WILL WAIT IN LINE TO USE IT.

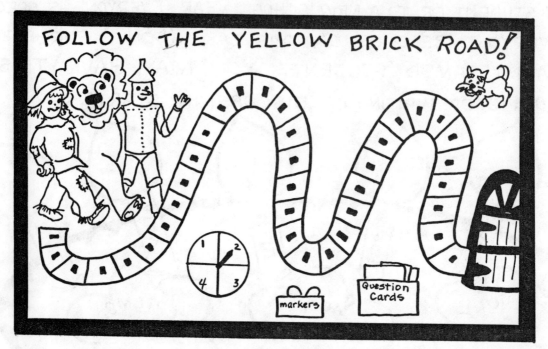

Pick a favorite theme for your grade level. Cut out or draw a pathway; tack to bulletin board. Attach a small piece of magnetic tape to each section, and to the markers. Add a spinner and a pocket full of question cards. Keep your gameboard open-ended so the cards can be changed to suit your immediate curriculum needs.

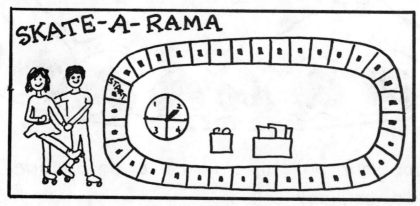